Quick-and-Easy
HEART-MOTIF QUILTS

Instructions and Full-Size Templates for Appliqué Projects

by Karen O'Do

Dover Publications, Inc., New York

This book is dedicated to my grandchildren,
who help me greet each day with a happy heart!

Acknowledgments

Special thanks to students, friends and family who contributed time, talent and enthusiasm to the heart-motif projects: Elsie Vredenburg, Estella Fessenden, Barb Durdle, Sue Bricker, Bertha Norman, Robyn Burradell, Louise Twyman, Judy Mayhak, Kathie DeJong, Kathleen Siegfried, Sue Gladstone, Debbie Fix, Susan Harry, Fanchion Stanger, Dorothy Fagerlin, Gayle Minkus, Darla Barnard, Linda Staudacher, Tamara Doane, Ann Trowbridge, Alice Stevens, Aileen Smith, Susan Yanusz, Marilyn Parr, Annette Jackman, Judy Strandquist, Jackie Huizen, Nancy Gillette, Mary Raushenberger.

Published in Canada by General Publishing Company, Ltd., 30 Lesmill Road, Don Mills, Toronto, Ontario.
Published in the United Kingdom by Constable and Company, Ltd.

Quick-and-Easy Heart-Motif Quilts: Instructions and Full-Size Templates for Appliqué Projects is a new work, first published by Dover Publications, Inc., in 1986.

Manufactured in the United States of America
Dover Publications, Inc., 31 East 2nd Street, Mineola, N.Y. 11501

Library of Congress Cataloging-in-Publication Data

O'Dowd, Karen.
  Quick-and-easy heart-motif quilts.

  (Dover needlework series)
    1. Quilting—Patterns.   2. Appliqué.   I. Title.   II. Series.
TT835.036 1986   746.9'7   86-6398
ISBN 0-486-25136-5

Introduction

One good thing leads to another, especially in quiltmaking. If one heart looks good, just think how two, three or even more will look! The heart shape is fun to work with; it has curves, a sharp point and a "valley"—all the different elements you are likely to come across in appliqué. You will find challenge and satisfaction with each design, yet the simplicity of each block will inspire you to keep up the good work and, perhaps, to add your own ideas as you go along.

Appliqué means to apply or sew pieces of fabric onto a larger "base" piece. The raw edges of the shapes to be sewn on are turned under so the sewing thread is drawn through a fold, rather than the fraying edge, to secure it to the base fabric. Good appliqué is accomplished with firm, invisible stitches; the curves are smooth, points are sharp and there are no frayed edges poking out.

This book is meant to successfully introduce people to quiltmaking so that they can feel good about their projects and about themselves, and to excite and challenge the more experienced quilter.

If you are a new quilter, you have no unlearning to do. There is no one-and-only way to make a quilt, so trust your own judgment as to one method being better than another. What works well for one person or project may not work at all for the next. Be sure you understand the instructions and techniques described, but use your mistakes as a source for information. Master the basic skills, but don't be obsessed with immediate perfection. Visualize the completion of the project. Relax, reflect and enjoy.

I would like you to fall in love with the idea of making a quilt with hearts, and to feel good about what you are doing—so good that you can't wait to finish the project. You shouldn't hurry, but with each finished block you should be eager to begin the next.

Most likely you are not interested in sitting down to read. You want to get started right now! Just for fun, cut out an assortment of fabric or paper hearts and arrange and rearrange them on a 15″ square of paper.

If you use a fabric "glue stick," you can glue an assortment of fabric hearts onto a fabric base and hang it where it can inspire you. Using felt or construction paper, or the "glue-basting" method, gives you an opportunity to try out new ideas quickly, without using a needle and thread.

Next, try a practice block, following the instructions on page 4. You should always make a practice block before beginning a whole quilt. This block should never be counted as one of the blocks to go into the quilt, because it is never really quite as lovely as you think it is. Take some time to read and reread the instructions for each block in the quilt. The practice block will let you know whether or not you enjoy appliqué by one method more than another. Appliqué techniques vary, so if at first you don't succeed, don't give up.

A good quilt makes you feel good when you look at it, and keeps you warm and feeling good when you cover up with it. Visions of grandeur often end up under rather than on the bed, so keep your ideas simple to begin with. A finished quilt is the best kind.

General Instructions

Assemble an assortment of sewing tools and supplies already on hand in your home, and keep them together in a sewing basket or shoe box. Included in your collection should be needles, thread, thimble, rust-proof straight pins and safety pins, ruler, pencils, pencil sharpener, good scissors for cutting fabric and not-so-good scissors for cutting out templates. Don't buy any new supplies until you have sorted through what you already have. Eventually you will need to purchase some items made especially for quilters, but all you need to get started are the items mentioned above, along with fabric and a good light to work in.

Most likely, polyester batting will be one of your purchases. There are many varieties to choose from, and experience will tell you which brand works best for you. You might also like to purchase some translucent plastic for making templates and some colored marking pencils. Quilting thread is widely available, but regular sewing thread coated with beeswax to keep it from knotting and tangling can be used.

A final must for quiltmakers: always work in good light and in a comfortable position.

All of the templates needed to appliqué the blocks shown are printed on heavy paper in the center of the book. To appliqué many of the blocks, you will need only the three basic heart shapes (*Templates A, B and C*). Because these three shapes are used so often, the templates for them need to be very sturdy. The translucent plastic top of a margarine tub (or any firm plastic you can see through) works very well for these templates. Place the plastic over the pattern and draw the heart design onto the plastic. Cut out the template using your not-so-good scissors. Make a template for each size heart. Feel free to change the size and shape of the hearts slightly so that they are the way *you* like them. You can also make templates for additional sizes of hearts for more variety. Punch a hole in each heart template near the point, and fasten them together with a safety pin. Take them apart when you work with a particular template size, then pin them back together again so they won't be easily lost.

If you have no plastic on hand, cut around the heart shapes just outside the printed lines. Paste or glue the shape onto a piece of lightweight cardboard or sandpaper, then cut out the heart shape on the lines.

LEARNING TO APPLIQUÉ

Making a Practice Block

The best way to learn how to appliqué is to actually try it, so choose a design that you would like to make as a practice block. To begin, choose a block that uses only the basic heart shapes, such as Blocks 1–4, Blocks 7, 8 and 12 and Blocks 35–40.

First cut a 15″ square of fabric for the base of the block and select the fabrics you will use for the appliqués.

Lay the heart template on the *right* side of the fabric and mark around the template with a sharp pencil so that you can see the lines. Cut out the fabric heart ¼″ outside the lines you drew. This extra ¼″ will be your seam allowance. It is not necessary that it be exact; for appliqué, the seam allowance should never be larger than ¼″, but smaller often works better.

With the right side of the fabric facing you, clip the material to the pencil line at the valley of the heart. Thread a fine needle with a single thread knotted at one end. Sewing from the bottom of the curve up to the valley, sew an even running stitch along the curved edge of the heart as close to the edge of the fabric as possible. These stitches will be turned under later so they will not show. Pull the thread gently, forming small gathers until the heart "cups" slightly. This "relaxes" the fabric so your curves will be smooth for the next step. Secure the thread by making a small backstitch, then cut the thread. Repeat on the other side.

With the right side of the fabric heart still facing you, turn the seam allowance toward the back with your fingers, beginning at the point. Turn the point under first; turn one side, then the other. Pinch or pin to hold in place. Be sure you turn the seam allowance far enough under so that the pencil marks do not show. Now you are ready to baste.

Thread a needle with a single thread about 18″ long; knot one end. Begin your basting stitches by piercing the fabric from the right side close to the edge of the fold. Leave all knots on the right side for easy removal of the basting stitches. Secure the seam allowance you pinned or finger-pressed by stitching all around the heart with a small running stitch. Baste as many hearts as your block calls for.

When the hearts are basted and ready to appliqué onto the base fabric, prepare the base by finger-pressing a crease diagonally from corner to corner, or horizontally and vertically as described in the individual block instructions. Do not iron in the creases. If the base fabric will not show or hold a crease, mark it lightly with a hard pencil, using a ruler for a guide.

Arrange the hearts on the base fabric following the diagram and instructions. Pin or glue-baste the hearts to the fabric. Place the block across the room, so that you can take a good look at it from afar. Rearrange the hearts until they look good to you, then check the arrangement with a ruler to verify the placement.

Appliqué the basted hearts using a fine needle and thread that closely matches the hearts. Use a blind stitch or a hemming stitch. Hide the knot under the heart or on the back of the base material. Come up from the back of the base material through the edge of the fold on the heart. Go back through the base material right next to the edge of the fold. Slant your needle and come up again

Diagram 1. *The blind stitch used for appliqué.*

through the base and folded edge of the heart about 1/16″ to 1/8″ away from the first stitch. Tug the thread gently so that the stitches are firmly in place and almost invisible. Don't pull too tightly, or the stitches will pucker.

Repeat this process until you have reached the valley of the heart. Tuck under any frayed edges or threads with your needle or fingernail. Take a few extra stitches if necessary to secure the raw edges, but if you take extra stitches in the valley of one heart, take them in all the hearts.

The stitches should be as close together as the fabric demands. If the fabric frays and is hard to keep in place, closer stitches are necessary. Secure your stitches with a backstitch or a small knot on the back of your work. Do not leave long tails of thread dangling; clean up your needlework on the back as well as the front of your piece.

Look at your work. Can you see your stitches? Are they loose on the front or the back? Are the fabrics lying flat? Are the curves smooth, and the points sharp? Sometimes the fabric seems to have a mind of its own, so don't always blame yourself if something goes wrong. Because this is a practice block, don't rip out stitches over and over, but go on to the next heart and the next. You will get better and better as you go along. Practice makes perfect.

Additional Tips for Appliqué

1. Choose your fabrics for appliqué carefully. Some fabrics either fray badly or are too bulky to work with. Fabrics that are 100% cotton are the easiest to work with.

2. Experiment with the grain line when cutting out the shapes to eliminate the need for clipping and easing, particularly on concave curves. Remember, though, that the look of the fabric is the most important.

3. To make the turning under easier, clip curves and trim points as necessary. Clip just to the pencil line, especially in the valleys.

4. Try glue-basting the cut-out fabric onto the base material without basting first, and turning under the seam allowance as you appliqué.

5. A small running stitch by hand or machine, rather than a blind stitch, also works well to attach the shapes to the base. Or you can embellish the appliquéd edge with embroidery stitches such as buttonhole or herringbone stitch in a contrasting color.

6. Sometimes only a few threads of fabric need to be turned under, using your fingernail or needle to "help" or "stroke" it under until you stitch it down.

7. To machine-appliqué, use a close satin stitch to completely cover the raw edges to sew them onto the base. Sometimes it is helpful to use an iron-on fusible interfacing before you cut out small shapes for machine-appliqué.

8. For perfect circles, cut a firm paper or light cardboard template. Cut a circle of fabric 1/4″ larger than the template. Run a double row of gathering stitches around the fabric circle near the edge. Lay the template on the wrong side of the fabric and pull the gathering thread tightly around the template as though you were covering a button. Iron flat, then pop out or cut out the template.

9. To draw large circles, use a compass or use a bowl, a plate or some other circular object as a guide.

10. To appliqué overlapping shapes, it is not necessary to turn under the seam allowance on the underlying pieces.

PLANNING YOUR QUILT

Planning is very important and can be done with pencil and paper to help avoid making mistakes that cost time and money and cause frustration. Good planning makes the construction and assembly of the quilt much easier. Pencils have erasers, and you can change plans on paper in a jiffy. Cutting up fabric without a plan can lead to a large scrap bag and not much success as a quiltmaker.

We have given you dimensions and fabric estimates for the quilts shown on the covers, but by adjusting the size of the borders and lattice, you can make a quilt perfect for your bed. Plan your quilt's dimensions and your own fabric requirements as dictated by the size of your bed and mattress. Measure from the floor on one side of your bed to the floor on the other side. This will be the absolute largest width your quilt can be. Jot down the smallest size that would satisfy you. Measure the length of your mattress and include extra length for going over and tucking under the pillow. Consider how far you want the quilt to drop over the end of the bed.

When you have decided on the size of your quilt, try drawing the quilt to scale using graph paper. A scale drawing will help you see how your plan is working. After your quilt is planned, you are ready to begin.

QUILTING YOUR PROJECT

A quilt is made of three layers, much like a sandwich. The top layer is beautiful, pieced or appliquéd or marked with a quilting design. The middle layer is soft and warm; most often polyester batting is used. The bottom layer, or backing of the quilt, is plain whole cloth. These three layers must be stitched together to keep the middle layer from moving around. The stitching that holds the three layers together is called quilting—a series of small, even running stitches, made down and up through all three layers.

I suggest that your completed appliqué blocks be "outline-quilted" around the outside of each shape. This way, you don't have to mark the fabric. When outline-quilting, sometimes two or three rows of "echo" quilting ⅛" to ¼" apart add extra emphasis. To mark other quilting lines on the base material, use a hard, sharp pencil and a very light hand.

To quilt a single block, make a textile "sandwich" of the appliquéd block, a square of batting and a square of backing. Beginning in the center of the block, baste through all three layers toward each corner. Sewing outward from the center to the corners eases out any wrinkles.

You may add horizontal and vertical rows of basting also, as well as a line of basting around the edges. The larger the block, the more basting is needed to keep the layers from slipping as you quilt. When you quilt a whole quilt without using a large quilting frame, the entire quilt is put together and basted in a giant textile sandwich exactly as you do with a single block.

After basting, the block is ready to be quilted in your lap, with or without an embroidery hoop or small quilting frame. Some people do extraordinary work without a hoop or frame, while others find them a necessity. Try each way and see what works best for you, but give each method a fair chance. Don't give up after a few stitches!

Thread a quilting needle with an 18" length of quilting thread, or a regular needle with regular thread that has been coated with beeswax. Quilting needles are short and sharp, ranging from size 7 to size 12. The lower the number, the larger the needle. Working with a variety of needles will help you decide what is comfortable and efficient for you. Tie a small knot on the long end of the single thread.

Insert the needle into the top layer of fabric about ½" away from where you choose to begin quilting. Bring the needle point up through the fabric exactly where you will quilt. Pull gently but firmly on the thread until the knot pops through the fabric and lodges in the batting. It takes a bit of practice to pop the knot through the fabric without breaking the thread, or pulling the knot all the way through, so keep on trying. No knots should ever show on the top or back of a quilt project. They would be the first thing to wear off, causing your stitches to unravel.

When the knot is safely concealed in the batting, you are ready to begin quilting. You will be sewing a small running stitch through all three layers of the "sandwich." It is important to keep one hand under the work so you can feel the needle as it pokes through from the top. If you are right-handed, the left hand remains under the work if you are quilting in a hoop or frame. When quilting without a frame, simply grasp the fabric sandwich with your left hand, allowing the helping finger to remain underneath. Obviously, reverse this procedure if you are left-handed, but experiment to see which is most comfortable for you.

The right hand does most of the work on top, with the left hand assisting below. A gentle "seesaw" rhythm is soon established. You may take one down-and-up stitch with your needle and pull the thread through, or you may put several stitches on the needle and then pull the thread through the fabric. To keep from getting tired, one thing you should avoid is the "stab" stitch—poking the needle down from the top with the right hand, then moving the right hand underneath to poke the needle back up.

Your stitches should be even, with the spaces the same size as the stitches. Eventually the stitches and spaces on the back should be the same size as the stitches and spaces on the top, but don't expect this to happen in the first few inches of quilting. From this point on in your quilting life you will always be looking for ways to make your stitches smaller, more even and more comfortable. Changing the angle at which you insert the needle can help, and changing the size of the needle you are using sometimes does the trick. Tightening or loosening your fabric sandwich in the frame can also be a factor.

As you quilt, pull the thread firmly, but not so tight that it puckers the fabric. To get from one area to another without ending your thread, insert the point of the needle into the top fabric, then run the needle through the batting to the spot where you wish to begin a new quilting line. Bring the point of the needle back up through the top fabric, and begin to quilt. Quilt until you run out of room to quilt, or until your thread begins to get alarmingly short. Plan ahead to end your quilting with no knots. Save one last stitch, which will be the final stitch to hide the knot. Before you take this last stitch, tie a small knot on the thread very close to the fabric. Sometimes two knots tied one on top of the other are more efficient than one. Take the last stitch through the top layer of fabric only. Run the needle through the batting as far as you can and bring it up through the top layer of fabric one more time. Pull the thread firmly until the knot is pulled through the fabric, then cut your thread at the point where it comes out of the top layer. The tail will pop back into the batting and be hidden, and your stitches will be secured by the hidden knot.

There are many ways to begin and end your quilting stitches. Watch other people and see how they do it. Sometimes you can begin quilting without a knot. Just pull your thread only halfway into the fabric, leaving a very long tail. Quilt in one direction until you run out of thread. End your stitching as described above, then thread your needle onto the tail you left when you started and quilt in the other direction.

Some quilters insist on beginning and ending their quilting with a small backstitch. As long as the backstitch cannot be easily seen when looking at your quilting, and as long as a tail is concealed in the batting, this is acceptable. Other quilters simply stitch back over a few stitches, then hide the tail of thread, but most often that can be readily detected. The objective in good quilting is to hold the layers together, to have small, even stitches and spaces, and to not have the beginning and ending quilting lines obvious and a distraction to the overall design.

Sore fingers can be taped, or special thimbles made of soft leather can be used underneath the quilt. There are several different "newfangled" thimbles to try on your right hand. Experiment to see what works best for you. All quilters develop interesting calluses on their fingers when they are quilting for long periods of time. The calluses are rather a status symbol!

If you get a spot of blood on a quilt, your own saliva and a small wad of quilting thread used right away will help to lighten the spot. The removal of stains is another interesting topic for discussion with other quilters, along with the hiding of knots and starting and stopping methods.

The look of your quilting is as personal as your penmanship. You may never be able to quilt in the neat, precise style of your neighbor, but neither do you sign your name in the same way she signs hers. Of course you should be working toward perfection, but relax and enjoy the beauty of the work you are doing, as long as you are doing your best. "Please yourself, then at least *one* will be pleased!"

Quilting on a Large Frame

Traditionally, a quilt was placed in a large frame for quilting. There is a wide range of quilting frames available today, both new and antique. Some are quite primitive, while others are fine pieces of furniture that tilt, raise and lower.

Four one-by-twos and four C-clamps from the local hardware store make a good basic quilting frame. The boards for the sides of the frame should be the length of the quilt plus about 8", and the top and bottom boards should be the width of the quilt plus about 8". Wrap the boards with strips of sturdy fabric (an old sheet works well for this) or staple or pin the fabric along the boards. You will pin or baste the quilt to this fabric.

Assemble the boards to form a large rectangle; put one C-clamp at each corner and tighten. Prop the frame on the backs of four kitchen or dining-room chairs.

Plan the quilt back to be at least 1" bigger all around than the top. Wrong side up, pin one edge of the backing to one fabric-wrapped quilting "stick" (quilters' slang for the one-by-twos) with safety pins or straight pins. Pull the fabric smooth and taut and pin the opposite side to the fabric on the other quilting stick. Leave the top and bottom edges free right now. Open and smooth out the batting on top of the backing. Pin the batting to the backing along the edges on the sticks. Now smooth the top onto the batting, right side up; pin into place along the wrapped sticks. Baste if you choose, but pins work well. If the free ends of the quilt sag, pin narrow strips of fabric to the edge, wrap them around the quilting stick near that edge and pin the loose ends to the edge of the quilt.

Quilting on the type of frame just described is begun along the edges, working in as far as you can reach comfortably. Then carefully remove the C-clamps along one side and roll the quilt up until you can begin quilting in another area. Replace the C-clamps, adjust the chairs to keep the quilt taut, and begin again.

Other quilting frames may have a different set of directions, and other quilters will have another approach to putting a quilt in a frame. Be a good listener or, better yet, offer to help someone put a quilt in a frame. It is an offer that is always appreciated, and it is by far the best way to learn.

An interesting substitute for a large quilting frame is a wooden card table with the top removed. Wrap the frame with fabric and you have an instant "mini" quilting frame at exactly the right height.

While working at a frame, get up and exercise a little bit every so often to keep from getting stiff. Roll your shoulders around, bend your neck and shake your hands to relax them. Good posture is important, and often the light and seating are a problem, so be sure that the lighting is good and the chair you choose is a comfortable height. Portable floor lamps and a long extension cord can be a big help.

Do try to stop in at quilting bees or demonstrations

where you can see people quilting. Don't be afraid to ask questions, but wait to be invited before you sit down in someone's place to quilt. You can learn a great deal by doing, so don't just sit there—quilt something!

Quilting "As-You-Go"

Not everyone has room for a large frame, nor is quilting on a frame always convenient.

Is it possible to make a professional-looking quilt without a frame? Of course it is! Many of the finest quiltmakers work without a frame. Quilting in your lap is very convenient, but grabbing a handful of king-size quilt is not quite as easy as grabbing a handful of one block. That is why many quiltmakers enjoy the "block-by-block" or "quilt-as-you-go" method. Each block is pieced or appliquéd, then quilted individually and set aside to be joined to other blocks later. After the quilted blocks are assembled, all that is left for the quilter to do is to bind the quilt.

When cutting the fabric for each block, the backing should always be at least ½" bigger all around than the top of the block; for example, with a 14" top, cut a 15" back. After quilting, the batting should be trimmed to be ¼" smaller all around than the top of the block. To keep the batting from getting ragged edges, pin the backing up over the raw edges of the top while you are quilting. Use small brass safety pins so you won't get stuck when you grab a handful of pins.

Baste the block and quilt as desired. Always stop the quilting at least ½" away from the raw edge of the block top to make joining the blocks possible. It is a good idea to mark the stitching lines you will be using to join the blocks before you begin to quilt.

When you have finished quilting the block, you may have to retrim the batting to be ¼" smaller than the finished top. You should have at least ½" of backing extending all around the edges. If the backing has somehow become crooked, simply trim the edges so that they line up better, but be careful to baste the next block more effectively. Wrinkles should be dealt with at the basting stage because it is very difficult to remove them after quilting unless you remove the quilting stitches.

To join two completed blocks, pin them, right sides together, along one edge. Stitch through two tops and one back, sewing with a ¼" seam allowance and starting and finishing ¼" from each edge. You will not catch the batting in the stitching if you have trimmed it properly.

Now open the two blocks out flat on the table with the backs facing upward. Fold the remaining unstitched edge under, so that the fold is even with the first stitching line; blind stitch this folded seam using thread to match the backing.

To assemble a whole quilt using this method, I would suggest sewing the blocks together in rows, then joining the rows using the same method, carefully matching seams. You can make a quilt in thirds or quarters, then join the sections this way. A quilt that is set together

using lattice or sashing is assembled in the same way, treating each lattice strip as an individual block. Borders are assembled in the same manner, then joined to the main body of the quilt. The quilt's edges should be bound as the very last step and the basting removed.

Remember, practice makes perfect, so it is usually best to start with a small project before attempting a full-size quilt.

HAPPY ENDINGS—
BINDING THE QUILT

Choices abound when the last step arrives. You can use purchased binding or make it yourself. You can use straight of the grain or bias* binding. You can turn under the corners of the binding or miter them.

Think of the options while you are preparing the quilt for binding. The projects shown on the covers all use hand-made, straight binding with the corners turned under, since I have found this to be the simplest and most satisfactory method. The width of the binding is up to you. I like to cut my binding 2½" to 3" wide (to finish to about ½" wide), but a narrower or wider binding might look better for certain projects.

Trim the ragged edges of the batting and backing so that they are even with the edges of the quilt top and there is ¼" to ½" of backing, batting and top beyond the stitching line to work with. Baste around the edge of the quilt through all three layers.

Cut a strip of binding the length of one side of the quilt plus 1". Fold the binding in half lengthwise with wrong sides together. Working from the top and matching raw edges, pin the binding to the right side of one edge of the quilt. Using a ¼" to ½" seam allowance (your choice), sew along the length of the binding, sewing through all three layers. It is perfectly acceptable to use a sewing machine for this, as long as you pin every few inches and sew carefully.

Turn the folded edge of the binding over the raw edges of the quilt to the back. An "empty" binding does not look or feel as good as a "full" one, so be sure that the seam allowance of the backing, batting and top extends into the binding. Blind stitch the folded edge of the binding to the back of the quilt, using thread that closely matches the binding. Do the two sides of the quilt first, trimming the ends of the binding even with the top and bottom. Before binding the top and bottom of the quilt, fold under ½" on each end of the binding strip. After the binding is complete, whipstitch the ends closed.

Please don't hurry when you get to the binding. It is exciting to be almost finished, but do a good, careful job. Try binding a single block to use as a wall hanging before trying a whole quilt. It pays to have a little experience.

Be sure you sign and date your quilt before you put it on your bed or send it out into the world.

Enjoy!

*For curved edges you *must* use bias binding; for straight edges you can use either straight or bias binding.

The Blocks
Blocks 1–12

In these blocks, heart motifs are arranged to form designs representing the 12 months of the year. Each design is based on a 13½″ finished block, although the size may be varied by using different size hearts or by moving the elements closer together or further apart. The colors given in the individual block instructions are those used to make the quilt shown. Feel free to use your imagination to create your own color scheme.

BLOCK 1
January—Snow Flowers

Crease the block horizontally, vertically and diagonally. Appliqué four brown-print large hearts *(Template A)* in the center of the block. Center the side hearts on the horizontal crease and the top and bottom hearts on the vertical crease. Appliqué a solid dark-brown large heart in each corner, placing it at least ½″ away from the raw edges to allow room for the quilting stitches.

Outline-quilt around the flower and the corner hearts.

This design is also lovely just quilted, with no appliqués. Simply trace around the template onto the fabric and quilt on the traced line. This could be particularly effective for winter with a white background and ice blue quilting thread.

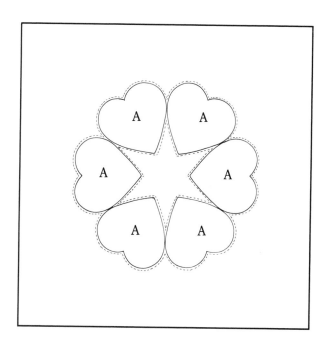

BLOCK 2
February—Hearts and Stars

Crease the block horizontally and vertically. Lightly draw an 8″-diameter circle in the center of the block. Arrange six rust-print large hearts *(Template A)* around the circle with the hearts touching at their widest point. The horizontal crease should run through the center of the side hearts and the vertical crease should fall between hearts. Use a ruler to make sure that all the hearts are the same distance from the center. Pin the hearts in place, then look at the block from a distance to check the placement of the hearts. Make any adjustments necessary, then appliqué the hearts in place.

Outline-quilt around the inner and outer edge of the "wreath" formed.

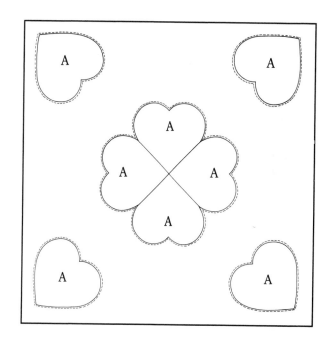

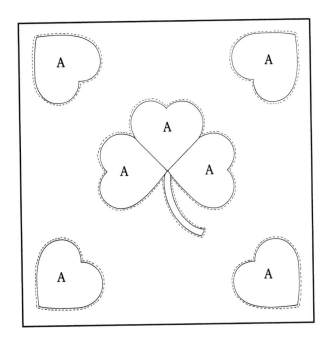

BLOCK 3
March—Hearts and Shamrocks

Crease the block horizontally, vertically and diagonally. Appliqué three brown-print large hearts *(Template A)* at the center of the block with the top heart centered on the vertical crease and the side hearts on the horizontal crease. For the stem, use a piece of brown bias tape, either purchased or made from a scrap of brown print. Appliqué a gold-print large heart in each corner, placing it at least ½″ away from the raw edges to allow room for the quilting stitches.

Outline-quilt around the shamrock and the corner hearts.

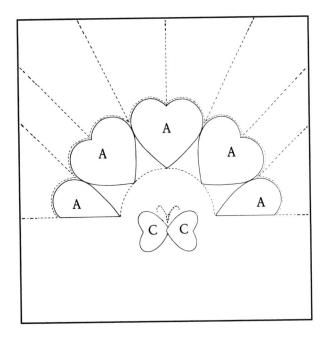

BLOCK 4
April—Under the Rainbow

Crease the block horizontally and vertically; make a second horizontal crease, 2″ below the first. Draw a semicircle on the block, having the top of the semicircle at the center of the block and the ends on the lower horizontal crease. Cut three large hearts *(Template A)* and two half large hearts from assorted beige, brown, rust and gold fabrics. Arrange the hearts around the semicircle, having the straight edge of the half hearts on the lower horizontal crease and the middle heart centered on the vertical crease. Look at the block from a distance to check the placement. Make any adjustments necessary and appliqué the hearts in place. Using a ruler, lightly draw a line from the valley of each heart straight out to the edge, and from between the hearts to the edge. For the butterfly, overlap the points of two rust-print small hearts *(Template C);* draw in the antennae.

Outline-quilt around the hearts and the butterfly and quilt along all traced lines, being careful to end the quilting ¼″ to ½″ from the edge of the block.

BLOCK 5
May—Flower Garden

Crease the block in half vertically and into thirds horizontally. Center a gold-print large heart *(Template A)* on the vertical crease with the point on the lower horizontal crease. Pin a rust-print large heart on either side of the gold heart. Center two beige-print large hearts with the points on the upper horizontal crease. Look at the block from a distance to check the placement of the hearts. Make any adjustments necessary, then appliqué the hearts in place. Lightly draw 2″-long stems on each flower and trace two small leaves *(Template D)* on each stem.

Outline-quilt around the hearts and quilt along all traced lines. The leaves could also be appliquéd.

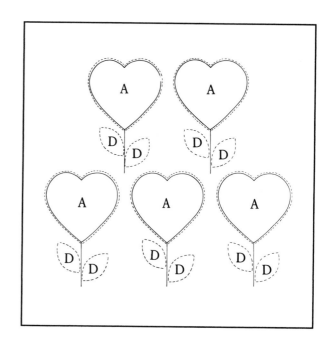

BLOCK 6
June—Bridal Wreath

Crease the block horizontally and vertically. Appliqué four beige-print large hearts *(Template A)* in the center of the block. Each heart should be centered on a crease and the points can meet or not as you choose. Using a large plate or embroidery hoop as a guide, lightly draw a 9¾″-diameter circle around the hearts to make the vine. Embroider the vine in chain stitch or herringbone stitch, or appliqué bias tape along the vine. Arrange ten dark-brown leaves *(Template E)* around the outside of the vine.

Outline-quilt around the center flower and around the leaves.

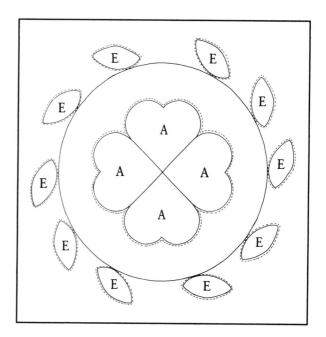

BLOCK 7
July—Starburst of Hearts

The radiating quilted lines of this block give the illusion of a Fourth of July firecracker.

Crease the block horizontally, vertically and diagonally. Arrange four rust-print large hearts *(Template A)* around the block, centering them on the horizontal and vertical creases. Arrange four solid dark-brown medium hearts *(Template B)* around the block, centering them on the diagonal creases. Look at the block from a distance to check the placement. Make any adjustments, then appliqué the hearts in place.

Outline-quilt around the hearts, then quilt from the center to the point of each heart.

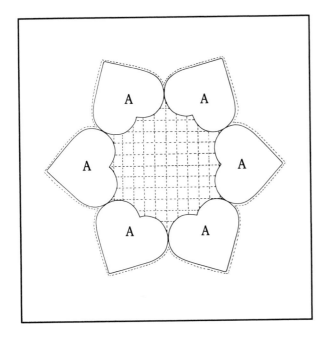

BLOCK 8
August—Sunflower

Crease the block horizontally and vertically. Arrange six gold-print large hearts *(Template A)* around the block, having the points out. The horizontal crease should run through the center of the side hearts and the vertical crease should fall between hearts. Look at the block from a distance to check the placement. Make any adjustments and appliqué the hearts in place. Using a ruler and a hard lead pencil, fill in the center of the flower with horizontal and vertical lines spaced ½″ apart.

To avoid having pencil marks on your block, use tape to mark the lines. Place a strip of masking tape on the flower with one edge along the center crease of the fabric. Quilt along the edge of the tape. Move the tape ½″ away and quilt along the edge. Repeat this process until the center is completely quilted with parallel lines. Cross these lines at a right angle with another strip of tape and repeat the process.

Outline-quilt around the outside of the sunflower.

BLOCK 9
September—Schoolhouse

From rust print, cut a 5¼″-by-5½″ rectangle and a 5¼″-by-6⅛″ rectangle to be used for the house; cut a 1¾″ square for the chimney (these measurements include the seam allowance). Cut the roof sections *(Templates F and G)* from rust print. Arrange the pieces on the block, leaving ¼″ between the house and roof sections; appliqué in place. Appliqué two solid-gold large heart *(Template A)* windows to the house. The windows could also be made in reverse appliqué by cutting the hearts out of the house pieces and turning under the raw edges.

Trace several small hearts *(Template C)* above the chimney for "smoke."

Outline-quilt around the house pieces and the windows; quilt along the traced lines.

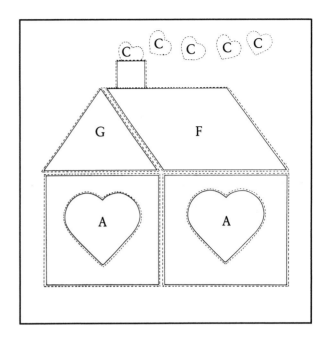

BLOCK 10
October—Mr. Punkin

Cut a large brown-print circle for the pumpkin (use a large hoop or plate for a template). From gold fabric, cut three medium hearts *(Template B)* for the nose and eyes. Cut five small hearts *(Template C)* for the mouth. Appliqué to pumpkin. Center the pumpkin on the block and appliqué; add a brown stem *(Template H)* to the top of the pumpkin.

Outline-quilt around the pumpkin and the features. Quilt a second row around the pumpkin, ⅛″ outside the first.

This design would also be effective using appliqués for the features, but quilting the pumpkin itself rather than appliquéing it.

Block 34 could also be used to symbolize October.

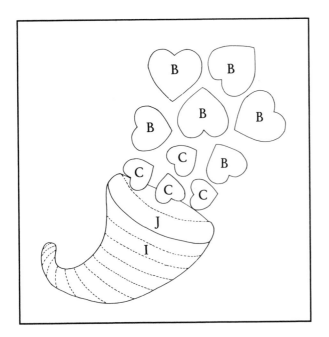

BLOCK 11
November—A Cornucopia of Hearts

Appliqué a solid brown cornucopia *(Template I)* with a gold lining *(Template J)* to the center of the block. With brown thread, embroider a line across the lining. Cut medium *(Template B)* and small *(Template C)* hearts from assorted rust, beige, brown and gold fabrics. Arrange them at random spilling out of the cornucopia. Appliqué the hearts in place.

Outline-quilt around the hearts and the cornucopia; with contrasting thread, quilt along the lines indicated on the cornucopia template.

For a special look, try stuffing the cornucopia lightly with a bit of batting before taking your final appliqué stitches. Or, experiment with other trapunto techniques.

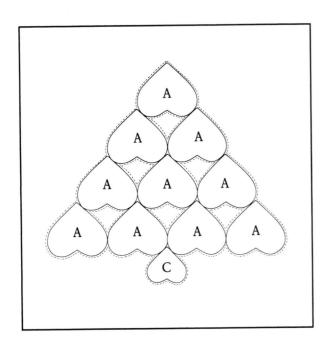

BLOCK 12
December—Tree of Hearts

Crease the block vertically. Cut large hearts *(Template A)* from brown print. Pin the hearts upside down on the block in rows, centering them vertically. Appliqué them in place. If you overlap the hearts you can use more rows; likewise you can use fewer hearts and top the tree with a "mini" heart and sprinkle mini-heart presents around the bottom of the tree. Add a brown small heart *(Template C)* for the trunk.

Outline-quilt around the hearts.

Blocks 13–24

Each of the following blocks was a winner in the 1982 Things Americana Quilt Block Contest. Each entrant was provided with a basic quilt block (finished size, 14″ square) and a piece of navy-print fabric. Entrants were required to use this fabric, the "fat heart" shape and primary colors to develop the hearts and flowers theme. As you will see, the winners expressed this theme in a variety of ways. Use our color suggestions or feel free to develop your own color scheme.

BLOCK 13
Hearts and Flowers Medallions
designed by Gayle Minkus

Crease the block horizontally and vertically. Lightly draw a 6½″-diameter circle in the center of the block. Arrange six navy-print medium hearts *(Template B)* around the circle, having the hearts ½″ apart at their widest point. The vertical crease should run through the center of the top and bottom hearts; the horizontal crease should fall between the side hearts. Use a ruler to make sure that the hearts are all the same distance from the center. Pin the hearts in place.

Cut six red pin-dot and six solid-yellow clamshells *(Template K)*. Turn under the seam allowance on the top edge only on the yellow clamshells; turn under the seam allowance on the red clamshells. Appliqué a red clamshell onto each yellow clamshell, leaving at least ¼″ of yellow showing at the top. Arrange the clamshells around the block about ½″ outside of the hearts, placing a clamshell between each pair of hearts; pin securely. Look at the block from a distance to check the placement of the motifs. Make any adjustments necessary, then appliqué the motifs in place.

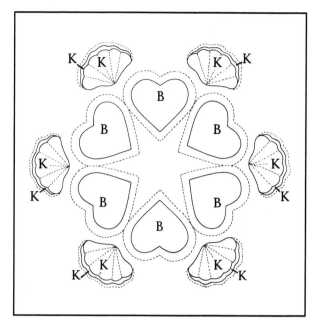

Outline-quilt around the hearts ¼″ away; the quilting lines of the hearts should just meet at their widest point. Outline-quilt around the top of the clamshells; quilt along the broken lines indicated on the template.

BLOCK 14
Overflowing Heart Basket
designed by Darla Barnard

Crease the block horizontally and vertically. The five red pin-dot medium hearts *(Template B)* in the basket are arranged first, overlapping them as shown. Place the top two hearts with the sides touching, then add the two side hearts. Center a heart on the vertical crease, with the valley of the heart on the horizontal crease. Appliqué these hearts in place.

Form the basket with three navy-print medium hearts. Appliqué the center heart first, then lap the two side hearts over it. Add two upside-down navy-print medium hearts for the basket base. Arrange five pale-yellow small hearts *(Template C)* on each side of the basket to form the handle; place a navy-print small heart at the top. Appliqué the handle in place. Appliqué two red pin-dot medium hearts on each side of the basket.

Using a contrasting color, outline-quilt around all hearts.

BLOCK 15
Outside Looking In
designed by Susan Harry

Four extra-large hearts, made of bias strips, intertwine to form an interesting shape in the center.

Crease the block horizontally and vertically. Place *Template L* with the broken lines on a crease and the point 6″ from the center; lightly trace around the template. Turn the template over, match the ends to the previous tracing and trace around again. Repeat this process three times to form four interwoven hearts. Each heart is made with two bias strips, starting and ending at the valley and point of the heart. Cut 1″-wide bias strips of red pin-dot and navy print. Press under ¼″ on each raw edge, then arrange the bias on the marked lines, having the navy hearts at the sides and the red hearts at the top and bottom. Weave the navy strips over the red strips near the center, then weave the red over the navy. Pin the strips securely and tuck the raw ends under at the point and valley of each heart. Trim the excess fabric from the raw edges and baste the strips in place. Appliqué the strips, sewing the inside curve first.

Pin a red pin-dot butterfly's body *(Template M)* in the upper left-hand corner; add red pin-dot and navy-print

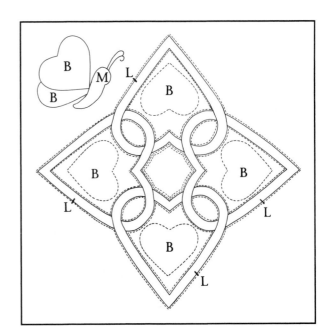

medium hearts *(Template B)* for wings. Appliqué in place. Embroider red outline-stitch antennae.

Trace a medium heart to the center of each woven heart; quilt along the traced lines. Outline-quilt around the woven hearts and the butterfly, very close to the edge.

BLOCK 16
Rain of Hearts
designed by Debbie Fix

Appliqué a row of four multicolored small hearts *(Template C)* in the lower right-hand corner of the block for flowers; lightly draw straight stems and trace tiny leaves *(Template D)*. Appliqué a row of four multicolored small hearts in the upper left corner for clouds; lightly draw raindrops (these could be tiny hearts). Draw a curve from the top of the left-hand cloud to the top of the right-hand flower. Repeat with the remaining clouds and flowers. Appliqué a navy-print large heart *(Template A)* sun and a white medium heart *(Template B)* bird with a red pin-dot small heart wing. Draw on beak, feet and tail feathers (these could also be appliquéd).

Quilt along all drawn lines with contrasting color thread; outline-quilt around all hearts, very close to the edge.

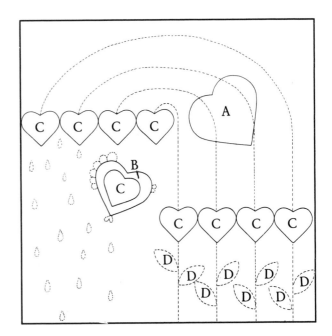

Blocks continue after template section.

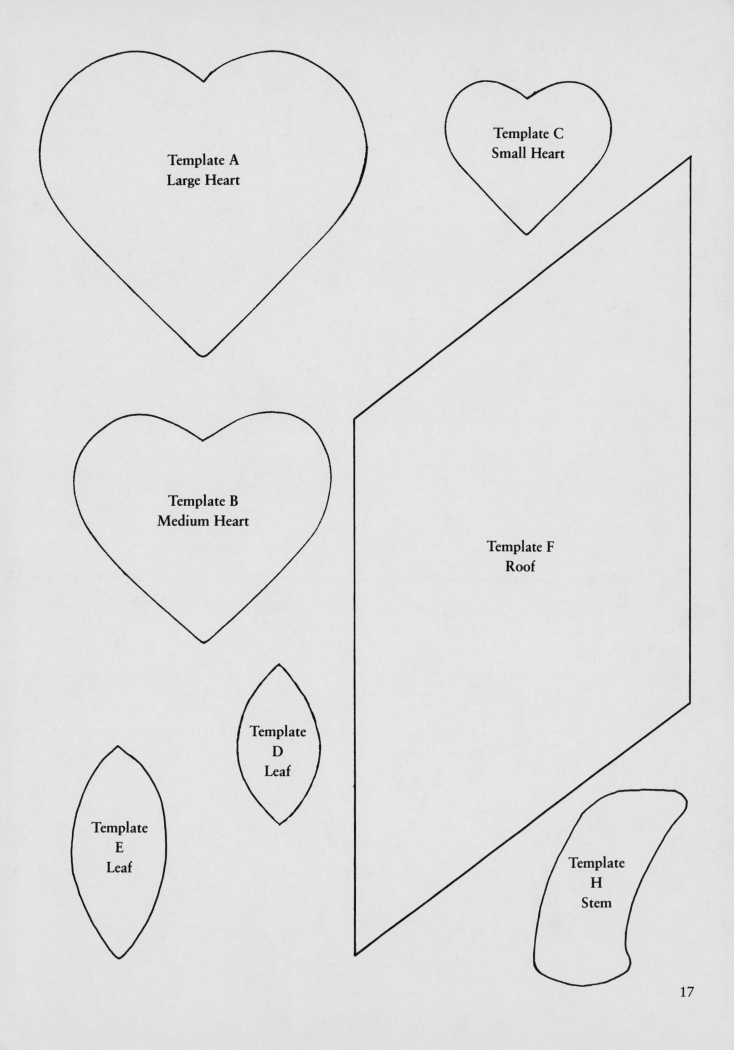

Template A
Large Heart

Template C
Small Heart

Template B
Medium Heart

Template F
Roof

Template
D
Leaf

Template
E
Leaf

Template
H
Stem

17

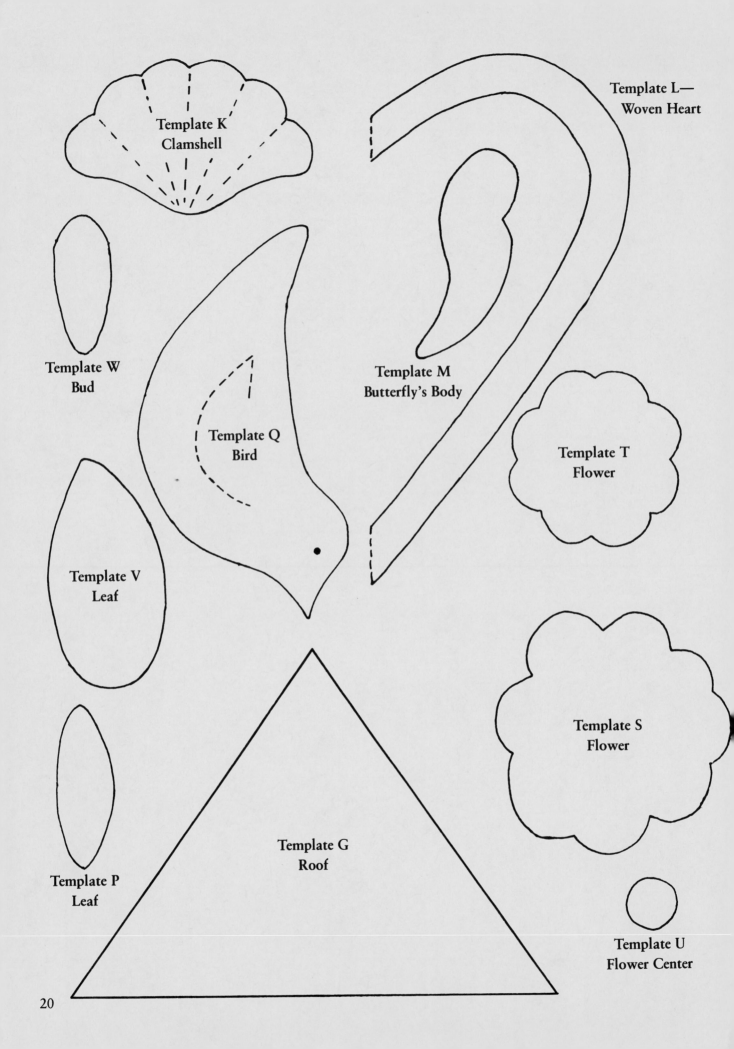

Template K
Clamshell

Template L—
Woven Heart

Template W
Bud

Template M
Butterfly's Body

Template Q
Bird

Template T
Flower

Template V
Leaf

Template S
Flower

Template P
Leaf

Template G
Roof

Template U
Flower Center

20

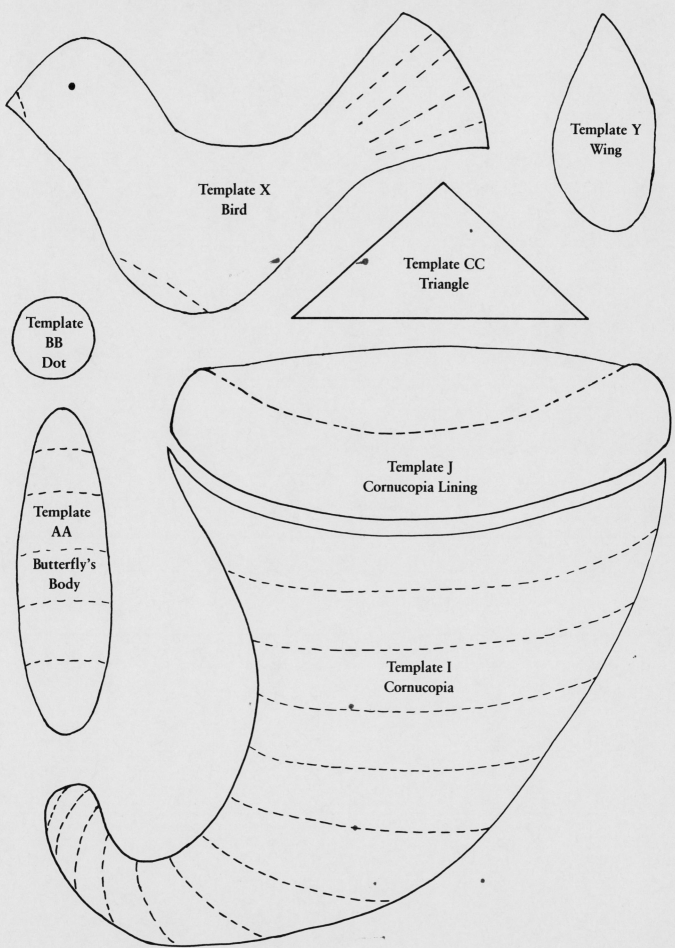

Template X
Bird

Template Y
Wing

Template CC
Triangle

Template
BB
Dot

Template
AA

Butterfly's
Body

Template J
Cornucopia Lining

Template I
Cornucopia

21

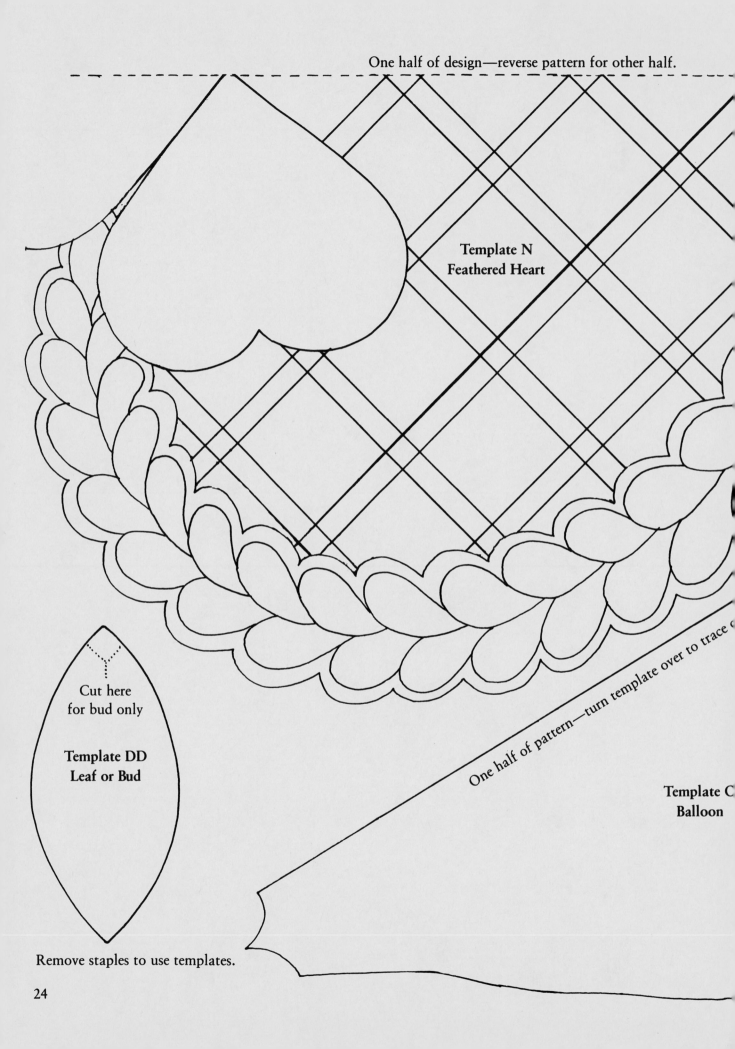

One half of design—reverse pattern for other half.

Template N
Feathered Heart

Cut here
for bud only

Template DD
Leaf or Bud

One half of pattern—turn template over to trace

Template C
Balloon

Remove staples to use templates.

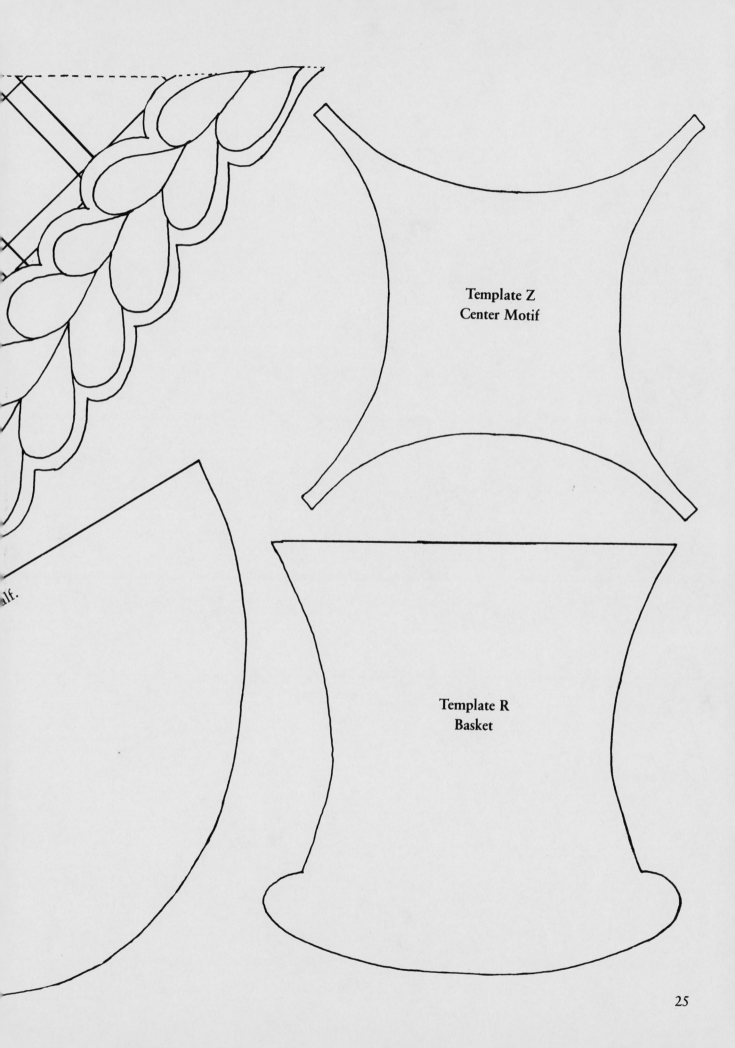

**Template Z
Center Motif**

**Template R
Basket**

alf.

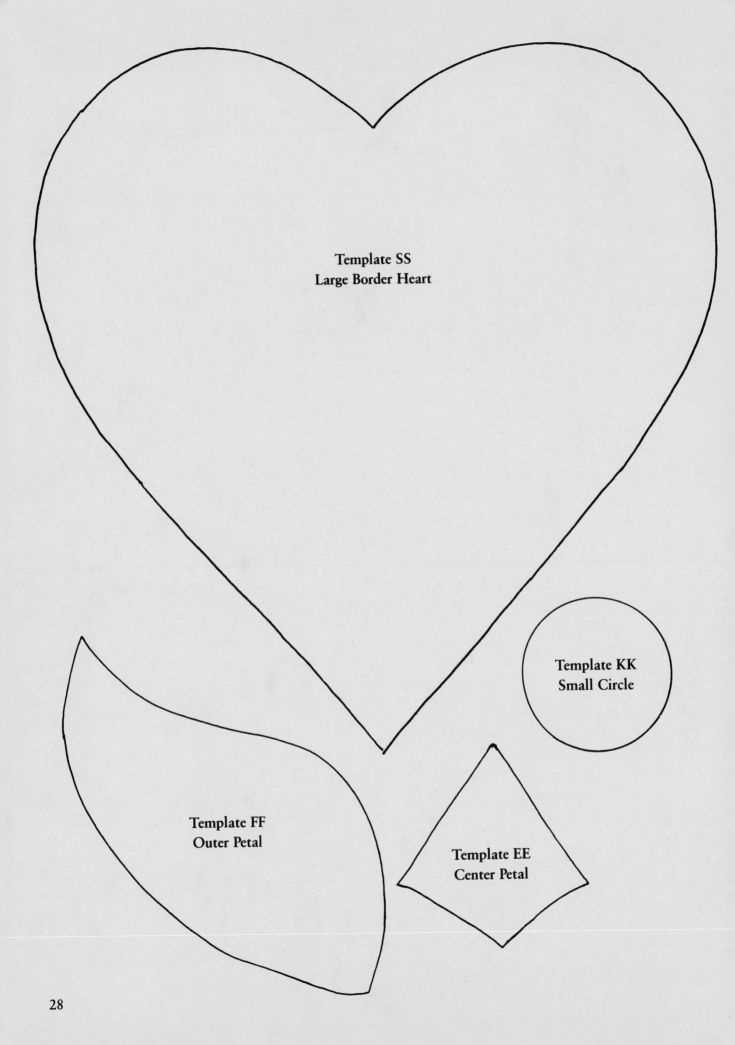

Template SS
Large Border Heart

Template KK
Small Circle

Template FF
Outer Petal

Template EE
Center Petal

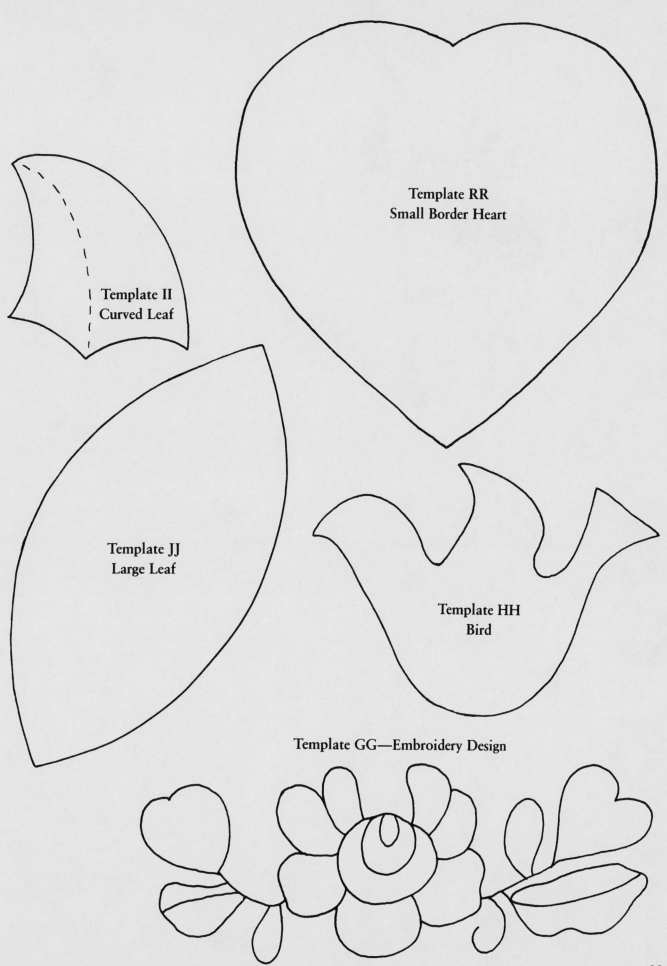

Template RR
Small Border Heart

Template II
Curved Leaf

Template JJ
Large Leaf

Template HH
Bird

Template GG—Embroidery Design

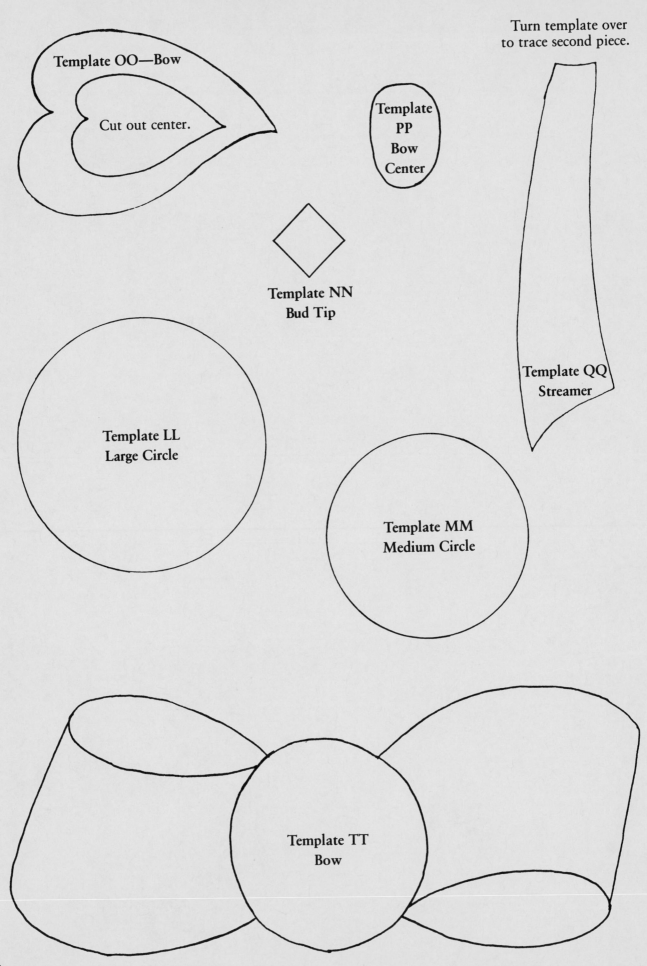

Template OO—Bow

Cut out center.

Template
PP
Bow
Center

Turn template over to trace second piece.

Template NN
Bud Tip

Template QQ
Streamer

Template LL
Large Circle

Template MM
Medium Circle

Template TT
Bow

32

BLOCK 17
Patchwork Heart
designed by Linda Staudacher

Three appliqué hearts form a shamrock at the top of a traditional quilted "feathered" heart.

One half of the feathered heart pattern is given *(Template N)*. Trace the design onto paper. Holding the pattern against a sunny window or an artist's light table, retrace the lines on the back of the paper so that you have both a left and a right side.

Crease the quilt block vertically. Slide the traced pattern under the block, matching the straight edge to the vertical crease; lightly trace the pattern, checking the diagonal lines with a ruler. Turn the paper over and trace the other half of the heart. Appliqué three navy-print large hearts *(Template A)* at the top of the feathered heart. With navy blue, embroider a small lazy-daisy stitch shamrock in each square in the center of the feathered heart.

Quilt along the center lines with white thread; quilt the feathered heart with contrasting thread.

BLOCK 18
Summer Flight
designed by Tamara Doane

String appliquéd hearts embellish a hot-air balloon.

Cut narrow strips in varying widths from an assortment of fabrics. Sew these strips with right sides together, using a ¼" seam allowance and angling some strips for more variety. Cut one large heart *(Template A)* and two half large hearts from the patched fabric; appliqué them to a red pin-dot balloon *(Template O)*. Appliqué the balloon onto the block at an angle. Cut a 2" square of yellow print for the basket and appliqué it in place.

Using the plastic lid of a margarine tub as a template, lightly draw semicircular clouds onto the block. With white thread, quilt along the "clouds" and outline-quilt around the balloon. With contrasting color thread, quilt down the balloon at the center (do not quilt through the heart) and between the hearts; quilt lines to the basket.

BLOCK 19
Buds in a Basket
designed by Ann Trowbridge

Crease the block horizontally and vertically. Pin two navy-print large hearts *(Template A)* on the block about 1″ below the horizontal crease, with the inner edges meeting at the vertical crease. Trace a large heart centered on the vertical crease with the point 2″ to 2½″ above the horizontal crease, then draw curved lines from the point of the heart down to the sides of the navy hearts to form the handle of the basket. Appliqué a green bias strip along the traced lines, tucking the raw ends under the navy hearts.

From red pin-dot, cut four 3″ squares. Right sides out, fold each square in half diagonally, then fold the side points to the center point to form buds. Pin the buds in place with the raw edges under the navy hearts; add four green leaves *(Template P)* around the buds. Appliqué the buds and leaves in place; appliqué the pinned hearts. Appliqué a navy-print large heart, upside down, between the first two navy hearts, then add a fourth navy-print large heart, right side up, on top of this heart. Appliqué a

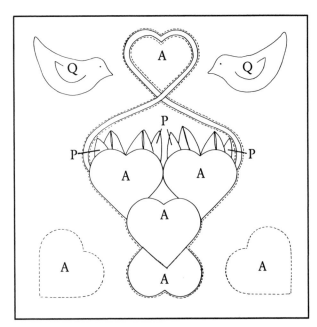

medium-blue-print bird *(Template Q)* on each side of the handle.

Trace a large heart in each lower corner of the block. Outline-quilt around the appliqués; quilt along the traced hearts and along the birds' wings.

BLOCK 20
Posies for Patricia
designed by Alice Stevens

This intricate flower basket has hearts peeking out of the multicolored bouquet.

Crease the block horizontally and vertically. Cut a brown basket *(Template R)*. From brown-striped fabric, cut three narrow strips; appliqué one strip down the center of the basket and one on each side of the center. Center the basket on the vertical crease, with the top on the horizontal crease; pin in place. Draw the handle onto the block and appliqué a brown bias strip along the drawn line. From the striped fabric, cut three strips 1″ wide and 12″ long. Fold the long raw edges of each strip to the center, then fold the strips in half lengthwise. Braid the strips together and pin them across the bottom of the basket, turning the ends under. Appliqué in place.

Cut flowers *(Templates S and T)* and flower centers *(Template U)* from assorted fabrics; cut green leaves *(Templates P and V)*. Arrange the flowers and leaves in the basket as desired. Cut several buds *(Template W)* and pin in place. Lap two small leaves over the lower end of each bud and add green bias stems. Tuck two navy-print medium hearts *(Template B)* and one large heart *(Tem-*

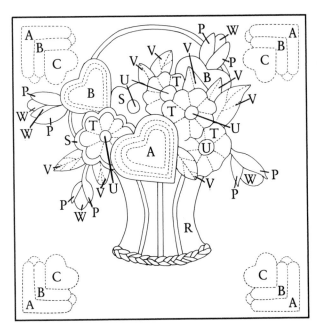

plate A) among the flowers. Appliqué all of the pieces to the block.

Trace overlapping small hearts *(Template C)*, medium hearts and large hearts in each corner of the block. Outline-quilt around the basket and flowers. Quilt along all traced lines; quilt along centers of leaves and flowers as desired.

BLOCK 21
Bluebird of Happiness
designed by Aileen Smith

Appliquéd bluebirds tug on quilted heartstrings, leading to an appliquéd heart.

Appliqué a navy-print large heart *(Template A)* just below the upper left corner of the block. Add three pale-blue birds *(Template X)* with navy-print wings *(Template Y)*.

Draw lines from the heart to the beak of each bird. Outline-quilt around all appliqués and quilt along the traced lines with contrasting thread. Try a "wavy" line of quilting on the heart strings to create the illusion of motion.

BLOCK 22
Heart-to-Heart
designed by Bertha Norman

Four appliquéd hearts are joined by a square with concave sides. A bold design is achieved by using only one dark print.

Crease the block horizontally, vertically and diagonally. Cut the center motif *(Template Z)* and four large hearts *(Template A)* from navy print. Place the center motif on the block with the corners on the diagonal creases; center a heart on each diagonal crease with the valley of the heart at a corner of the center motif. Appliqué the pieces to the block.

Trace a medium heart *(Template B)* between each pair of large hearts, centering each heart on a horizontal or vertical crease. Using white thread, outline-quilt around the center motif and the large hearts; quilt diagonally from corner to corner of center motif. With navy thread, quilt the traced hearts, then quilt again ¼″ outside the first quilting.

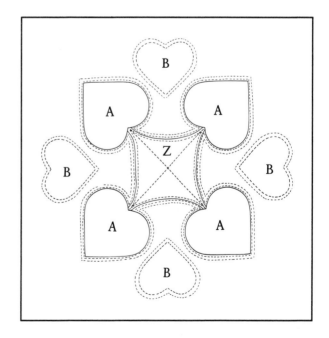

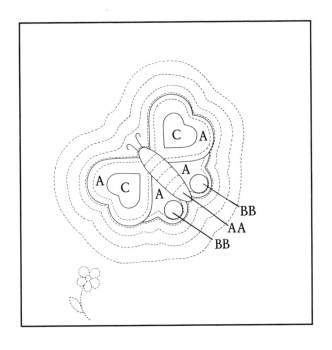

BLOCK 23
May Butterfly
designed by Susan Yanusz

Heart-shaped wings, embellished with hearts and circles, are given extra dimension with a bit of trapunto.

Pin a pale-yellow butterfly's body *(Template AA)* to the block; add four yellow-print large hearts *(Template A)* for wings. Appliqué the pieces to the block, stuffing them lightly. Appliqué navy-print small hearts *(Template C)* and dots *(Template BB)* to wings. Embroider yellow outline-stitch antennae.

Draw a small flower below the butterfly on the left. Quilt across the butterfly's body as indicated by the broken lines on the template. Outline-quilt around the butterfly and inside the large hearts; stitch two more rows of echo quilting around.

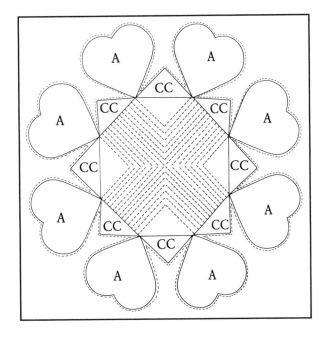

BLOCK 24
Hearts and Diamonds
designed by Judy Mayhak

Eight hearts appliquéd alternately with eight triangles form an interesting design highlighted by rows of echo quilting.

Crease the block horizontally, vertically and diagonally. Place a yellow-print triangle *(Template CC)* on each crease, with the center points out and the side points touching. Add a navy-print large heart *(Template A)* between each pair of triangles. Look at the block from a distance to check the placement of the motifs. Make any adjustments necessary, then appliqué the pieces to the block.

Quilt along the diagonal creases in the center of the block, dividing the center into quarters. In each quarter, quilt additional rows of diagonal lines to form triangles, spacing the rows 1/4″ apart. Outline-quilt around the hearts and the outer edges of the appliquéd triangles.

Block 25

Bridal Wreath Variation

This version of the popular bridal-wreath pattern is based on a 22″ block, although it could easily be made smaller using the medium or small hearts rather than the large heart.

Crease the block horizontally, vertically and diagonally. Using a 14″-diameter embroidery hoop as a guide, lightly draw a circle on the block for the vine. Embroider the vine in chain stitch, using 3 strands of green embroidery floss. Appliqué two red-print and two solid-red large hearts *(Template A)* in the center of the block, having the points toward the center and hearts of identical fabric diagonally opposite one another. Appliqué nine solid-green leaves *(Template DD)* evenly spaced around the inside of the embroidered circle. Appliqué six solid-green and six green-print leaves around the outside of the embroidered circle, alternating the solid and print leaves. Appliqué a print or solid large heart in each corner, having hearts of identical fabric diagonally opposite one another.

Outline-quilt around the hearts.

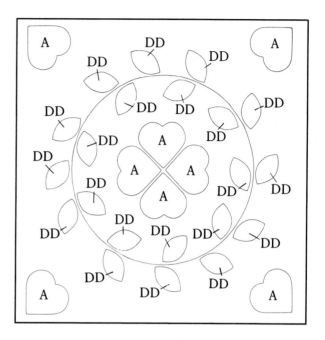

Blocks 26–28

In these three blocks, the hearts are combined with other simple shapes to form a variety of spring flowers. A mixture of different techniques, from machine appliqué to hand embroidery, adds special interest to the designs.

BLOCK 26
Sweetheart and Tulips
designed by Annette Jackman

This block is machine appliquéd using contrasting color thread.

Pin two navy-print center petals *(Template EE)* and four yellow-print outer petals *(Template FF)* to the block to form two tulips. Add two green-print bias strips for stems and two medium hearts *(Template B)* for leaves. Work a close machine satin stitch around all pieces, using green thread for the tulips and yellow thread for the stems and leaves.

Outline-quilt around all appliqués; quilt leaves as indicated on the diagram.

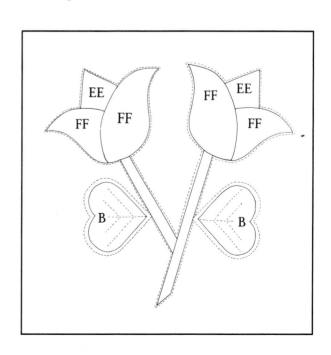

BLOCK 27
Symbols of Love
designed by Judy Strandquist

Crease the block vertically, horizontally and diagonally. Arrange four navy-print large hearts *(Template A)* around the center of the block, having a heart on each diagonal crease and having points about ½″ from the center of the block. Appliqué the hearts in place. Trace the embroidery design *(Template GG)* onto a sheet of white paper; turn the paper over and retrace the lines on the back. Slip the paper under the block, centering the design on a horizontal or vertical crease, halfway between the center hearts and the edge of the block. If the lines are hard to see, tape the paper and the fabric to a sunny window or an artist's light table. Trace the design onto the fabric. Repeat on each side of the block, reversing the design on two sides. Using three strands of embroidery floss, embroider the design in satin stitch and outline stitch, working the large flower in four shades of blue, the small flower in gold and the stems and leaves in two shades of green. The design would also be effective appliquéd or quilted.

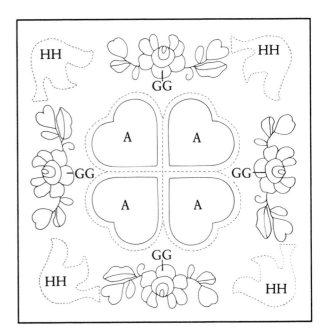

Trace a bird *(Template HH)* onto each corner of the block. Outline-quilt around the hearts. Quilt along the traced lines.

BLOCK 28
"Flower of Hearts"
designed by Jackie Huizen

Crease the block horizontally and vertically; make a second horizontal crease 1½″ above the center. Arrange four navy-print large hearts *(Template A)* on the block, centering the top and bottom hearts on the vertical crease and the side hearts on the top horizontal crease; pin securely. Add a green pin-dot curved leaf *(Template II)* to each of the top three hearts and a green pin-dot stem to the lower heart. Pin two green pin-dot large leaves *(Template JJ)* to the base of the stem. Appliqué the pieces to the block. Pin four red-print small hearts *(Template C)* on top of the large hearts, centering the small hearts between the large hearts; appliqué them to the block. Appliqué a solid-gold small circle *(Template KK)* to the center of the flower.

Outline-quilt around all pieces; quilt down the center of each leaf.

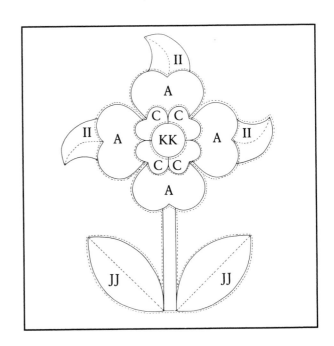

Blocks 29 and 30

The rose is one of the most popular motifs found in the traditional appliqué quilt and numerous versions exist. The names of some versions, such as the Rose of Sharon, were biblical in origin; some, like the Whig Rose and the Democratic Rose, were politically inspired; while still others, like those shown here, were named for their place of origin. All of these designs are similar, having a central blossom surrounded by symmetrically placed leaves or buds. In these two blocks the rose itself is formed by four hearts with two circles at the center.

BLOCK 29
Lancaster Rose

Crease the block diagonally. For the rose, cut four light-colored large hearts *(Template A)* and four darker-colored medium hearts *(Template B)*. Appliqué a medium heart on top of each large heart to form the petals. Arrange the petals on the block with the points touching and the hearts centered on the creases; pin in place. For the leaves, slip a large heart, with the point out, under each petal. Appliqué these pieces in place. Appliqué a dark-colored medium circle *(Template MM)* onto a lighter large circle *(Template LL)*; then appliqué the large circle to the center of the rose.

Outline-quilt the rose and the leaves.

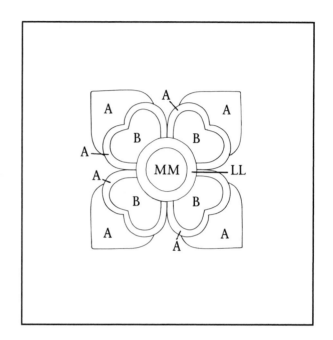

BLOCK 30
Ohio Rose

Crease the block diagonally. For the rose, cut four light-colored large hearts *(Template A)* and four darker-colored medium hearts *(Template B)*. Appliqué a medium heart on top of each large heart to form the petals. Arrange the petals on the block with the points touching and the hearts centered on the creases; pin in place. Cut four light-colored buds *(Template DD)* and cut along the dotted lines indicated on the pattern. Pin a darker tip *(Template NN)* underneath the top of each bud; appliqué in place. Pin a bud at the valley of each heart. Arrange two leaves *(Template DD—the same template is used for both the buds and the leaves)* at the base of each bud with the lower points of the leaves under the hearts. Appliqué all of these pieces to the block. Appliqué a dark-colored medium circle *(Template MM)* onto a lighter large circle *(Template LL)*; then appliqué the large circle to the center of the rose.

Outline-quilt the rose, buds and leaves.

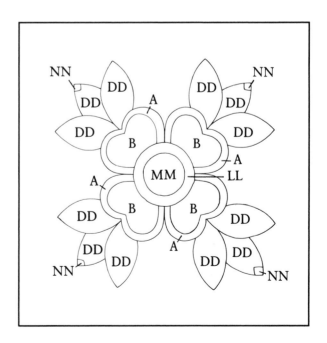

Blocks 31–33

Gather a bouquet of hearts and tie them with a bow, or tie the hearts themselves into a bow to create these spring-like designs.

BLOCK 31
May Bouquet

Crease the block horizontally and vertically. Scatter five medium hearts *(Template B)* across the upper portion of the block and appliqué them in place. Draw stems from the point of each heart, having all the stems cross about 1½″ to 2″ below the center of the block. Embroider the stems in outline or chain stitch, or appliqué bias tape along the lines. Add leaves *(Template E)*. Using 2″-wide ribbon, tie a bow and tack it over the intersection of the stems.

Outline-quilt around the hearts.

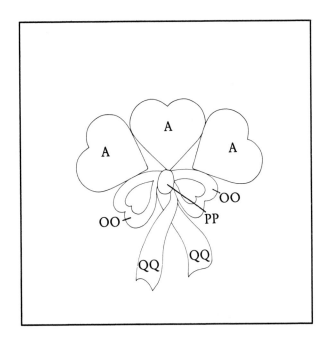

BLOCK 32
Trio of Hearts

Crease the block horizontally and vertically. Pin a large heart *(Template A)* on the vertical crease with the point on the horizontal crease. Add a large heart on each side of the center, tilting these hearts. Cut two bows *(Template OO)*, one bow center *(Template PP)* and two streamers *(Template QQ)*. Arrange the two bow pieces and the streamers below the hearts and appliqué all of the pieces to the block. Appliqué the bow center in place.

Outline-quilt all the appliqué pieces.

BLOCK 33
Shamrock Heart

Crease the block horizontally and vertically. Make a second horizontal crease about 1″ to 1½″ above the first crease. Arrange three large hearts *(Template A)* on the block with the points touching, having the top heart on the vertical crease and the side hearts on the upper horizontal crease. Appliqué the hearts to the block. Cut two streamers *(Template QQ)* and appliqué in place. Appliqué a small circle *(Template KK)* over the points of the hearts and the top end of the streamers.

Outline-quilt all of the appliqué pieces.

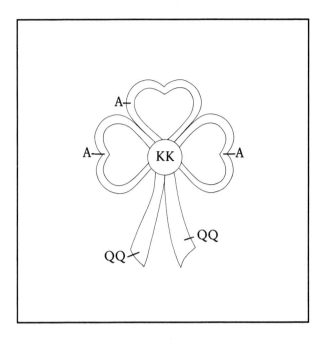

Block 34

Circle of Hearts

Crease the block diagonally. Arrange four large hearts *(Template A)* on the block with the points touching, centering each heart on a crease. Appliqué the hearts to the block. Using a plate or a large hoop as a guide, lightly draw a circle around the hearts. Arrange eight small hearts *(Template C)* around the circle with the points running counterclockwise. Appliqué the hearts in place.

Draw a curlicue between each pair of hearts. Outline-quilt around the center flower and the small hearts; quilt along the drawn lines.

Blocks 35–40

In this last group of blocks, the hearts are arranged and rearranged to form a series of complex symmetrical designs, similar to those created by a kaleidoscope.

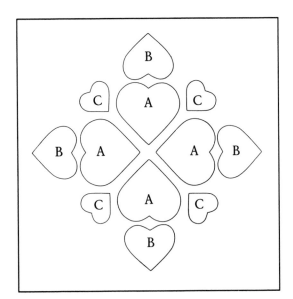

BLOCK 35
Diamond Medallion

Crease the block horizontally, vertically and diagonally. Arrange four large hearts *(Template A)* on the block with the points about ¼″ from the center, having each heart centered on a horizontal or vertical crease. Just beyond these hearts, center medium hearts *(Template B)* on the horizontal or vertical creases with the points out. Center a small heart *(Template C)* on each diagonal crease with the point close to the large hearts. Appliqué the hearts to the block.

Outline-quilt around the hearts.

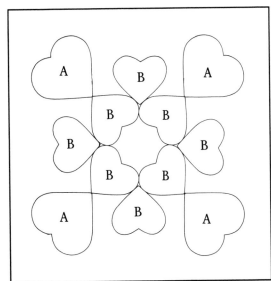

BLOCK 36
Figure Eights

Crease the block horizontally, vertically and diagonally. Arrange four medium hearts *(Template B)* on the block, having the points out and the hearts centered on the diagonal creases. The hearts should just touch at the center. Center a large heart *(Template A)* on each diagonal crease, with the point touching the point of the medium heart. Center a medium heart on each side on the horizontal and vertical creases, with the points between the center medium hearts and the sides touching them. Appliqué the hearts to the block.

Outline-quilt around the outer edge of the shapes formed and around the center opening.

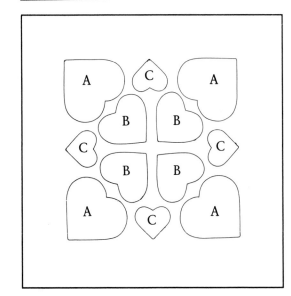

BLOCK 37
Square Medallion

Crease the block horizontally, vertically and diagonally. Arrange four medium hearts *(Template B)* on the block with the points about ½″ from the center, having the hearts centered on the diagonal creases. On each diagonal crease, just outside the medium hearts, center a large heart *(Template A)* with the point out. Center a small heart *(Template C)* with the point out on each side on the horizontal or vertical crease. Appliqué the hearts to the block.

Outline-quilt around the hearts.

BLOCK 38
Wreath of Hearts

Crease the block horizontally, vertically and diagonally. Arrange four small hearts *(Template C)* on the block with the points out, centering each heart on the horizontal or vertical crease. The hearts should just touch at the center. Using a plate or a large hoop as a guide, lightly draw a circle around the hearts. Place a large heart *(Template A)* on each side, centering it on a vertical or horizontal crease and having the point on the circle. Center a large heart on each diagonal crease, having the *top* of the heart on the circle. Appliqué the hearts to the block.

Outline-quilt around the inner and outer edge of the two wreaths formed.

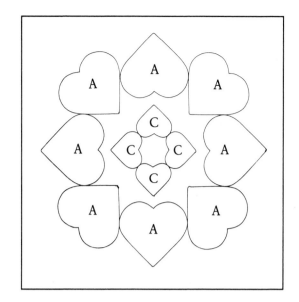

BLOCK 39
Heartsease

Crease the block horizontally, vertically and diagonally. Arrange four medium hearts *(Template B)* on the block with the points touching, centering the hearts on the diagonal creases. Center a large heart *(Template A)* on each diagonal crease, having the point touching the valley of the center heart. Place a medium heart on each side, centering it on a horizontal or vertical crease and having the top of the heart touch the tops of the center hearts. Appliqué the hearts to the block.

Outline-quilt around the hearts.

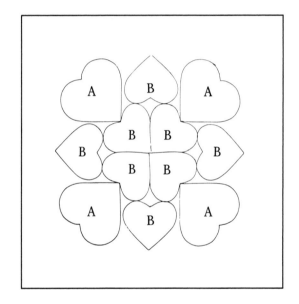

BLOCK 40
Kaleidoscope

Crease the block horizontally, vertically and diagonally. Arrange four small hearts *(Template C)* on the horizontal and vertical creases with the points out. Place a medium heart *(Template B)* on each side with the valley of the medium heart touching the point of the small heart. Place a small heart at top and bottom, with the point touching the point of the medium heart. On the sides, place a small heart with the *valley* touching the point of the medium heart. Center a medium heart on each diagonal crease with the point in; place a small heart just outside this heart with the point out and the top of the small heart touching the top of the medium heart. Appliqué the hearts in place.

Outline-quilt around the hearts.

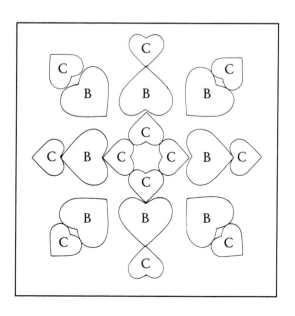

Heart Motif Projects

The heart motif blocks shown on the previous pages can be used to make an almost endless variety of projects, ranging from full-size quilts to pillows to wall hangings and more. For inspiration, we have pictured two full-size quilts, one "mini" quilt and a wall hanging on the covers of the book. The instructions for these items are given below.

The measurements given here are guidelines only. Adjust the size of the lattice strips and borders to make the quilt the size you need.

Block-of-the-Month Quilt

Approximately 76" by 93"

Materials Needed: 45"-wide cotton or cotton-blend fabrics—10 yds. of muslin for the blocks and backing, 3½ yds. of dark brown print for the borders, lattice strips and appliqués, 2 yds. each of rust print and gold print for the borders and appliqués, 1½ yds. of solid dark brown for the corner squares, accent squares, binding and appliqués and scraps of beige print and solid gold for the appliqués.
90"-by-108" quilt batting.
Sewing thread to match fabrics.
Dark brown quilting thread.
Lightweight cardboard.

Our sample quilt was made of an assortment of earth-tone fabrics on a muslin background. We chose to use the "quilt-as-you-go method"—quilting each block separately, then setting the blocks together with lattice strips. See page 8 for assembling, quilting and joining quilt-as-you-go blocks.

Cut cardboard templates for a 13½"-square quilt block, a 3"-by-13½" lattice strip, a 3" accent square and a 12" corner square. To use the templates, trace around them on the *wrong* side of the fabric. When cutting out the pieces, leave at least ¼" seam allowance around.

From brown print, cut two long borders 5½" by 69½" and two short borders 5½" by 53"; mark and cut thirty-one lattice strips. From rust print, cut two long borders 4½" by 69½" and two short borders 4½" by 53". From gold print, cut two long borders 3½" by 69½" and two short borders 3½" by 53". From solid dark brown, trace and cut four corner squares and twenty accent squares; cut 2½"-wide strips to piece two 94" long strips and two 78" long strips for binding. From muslin, trace and cut twelve quilt blocks.

Make and quilt the blocks following the individual block instructions for Blocks 1–12. Assemble sixteen lattice strips with batting, backing and top, and quilt each, ½" from the edges. Following the Assembly Diagram, arrange Blocks 1, 2 and 3 in a row, having a quilted lattice strip between each pair of blocks and at each end of the row. Matching the traced lines carefully, sew the blocks and strips together. Repeat with the remaining blocks and quilted strips to make four rows of three blocks each.

Now join three lattice strips end to end with an accent square between each pair of strips and at each end of the row. Trace a small heart *(Template C)* to the center of each accent square. Back the row and quilt on the traced lines and around each short strip ½" from the sides and ¼" from the ends. Repeat with the remaining lattice strips and accent squares to form five rows in all.

Pin a row of lattice strips to the top of the first row of blocks, matching seam lines and seams very carefully. If something doesn't fit, now is the time to make adjustments. Sew the strip to the blocks and set aside. Repeat with the remaining rows of blocks. Now, join all of the rows together, finishing with the last row of lattice strips and accent squares at the bottom.

To assemble the wide borders, sew a gold border to one long edge of a rust border, then sew a brown border to the other long edge of the rust border. Repeat with the remaining borders to make two long and two short borders. Back each wide border and quilt ½" from each raw edge and ¼" from each seam.

Following the instructions for Block 8, trace the sunflower motif on each corner square (*do not appliqué*). Back the square and quilt along the traced lines. Sew a corner square to each end of each short border. Sew the long borders to the sides of the quilt and the short borders to the top and bottom.

Bind the quilt with brown *(see page 8)*.

Hearts and Flowers Quilt

Approximately 82″ by 100″

Materials Needed: 45″-wide cotton or cotton-blend fabrics—6 yds. for the back (we used the same navy print used for the borders), 5 yds. navy print for the borders, lattice strips and appliqués, 2½″ yds. solid white for the blocks, 2 yds. yellow print for the borders and appliqués (1¼ yds. if the border is pieced), 1½ yds. red pin-dot for the accent squares, binding and appliqués; scraps of medium blue, green, pale yellow and white prints, brown stripe and solid blue, pale blue, green, pale yellow, bright yellow and brown.
90″-by-108″ quilt batting.
Sewing thread to match fabrics.
White, navy, yellow, red and green quilting thread.
Small amount of navy, yellow and red embroidery floss.
Cardboard for templates.

Cut cardboard templates for a 14″-square quilt block, a 3″-by-14″ lattice strip and a 3″ accent square. To use, trace around the template on the *wrong* side of the fabric. When cutting out pieces, leave at least ¼″ seam allowance around.

Trim the selvages from the backing fabric. Cut the fabric into two 3-yd. lengths and sew them together along one long edge. From navy print, cut two 12½″-by-99½″ and two 12½″-by-75½″ border strips; trace and cut thirty-one lattice strips. From yellow print, cut two 2½″-by-71½″ and two 2½″-by-58½″ border strips (borders may be pieced if necessary). From red pin-dot, cut 3″-wide strips to piece two 84″-long and two 102″-long strips for binding; trace and cut twenty accent squares. From white, trace and cut twelve quilt blocks.

Construct the blocks following the individual block instructions for Blocks 13–24. To set the quilt together, arrange three blocks in a row following the Assembly Diagram, having a lattice strip between each pair of blocks and at each end of the row. Right side in, pin the blocks and lattice strips together, matching marked lines; stitch. Repeat with the remaining blocks to form four rows of three blocks each. In the same manner, join three lattice strips end to end with an accent square between each pair of strips and at each end of the row. Repeat with remaining lattice strips and accent squares to form five rows.

Pin a row of lattice strips and accent squares to the top of the first row of blocks, matching seam lines and seams very carefully. If something doesn't fit, now is the time to make adjustments. Sew the sections together and set them aside. Repeat with the remaining rows of blocks. Now join all the rows together, finishing with the last row of lattice strips and accent squares at the bottom.

Pin the long yellow border strips to each side of the joined blocks, pinning every 2″ at right angles to the sewing line. Be sure that there is no stretching or moving of the fabric. Stitch, being careful to make the seams straight. Trim excess seam allowance. Do not press seams open, but press them to one side (toward the darkest fabric whenever possible). Remove and trim any extra thread. Stitch the short borders to the top and bottom in the same manner.

Cut fourteen small border hearts *(Template RR)* from assorted print fabrics. With pins or a pencil, mark across the center of each short navy border; mark three more lines on each side of center, spacing them an equal distance apart. Appliqué a small border heart on the center line; then working out toward the end on each side, skip the next line and appliqué a heart on the next line. Trace an upside-down heart centered on each remaining line. Mark the long navy borders in the same way, marking four lines on each side of the center. Skip the center line and appliqué a heart on the line to either side of center. Complete as for the short borders. Trace an upside-down heart to each remaining line. Pin the short borders to the top and bottom of the quilt with the hearts pointing out; sew them in place. Pin and sew the long borders to the sides. Make strip patchwork fabric as for Block 18 and cut four large border hearts *(Template SS)*. Sew a heart to each corner of the border.

Assemble the quilt top, the batting and the backing *(see page 6)*. Quilt each block as described in the individual instructions. Outline-quilt around the border hearts and ¼″ from the seamlines in the border, lattice strips and accent squares. Quilt the marked hearts in the borders.

Bind the quilt with red pin-dot *(see page 8)*.

Bridal Wreath "Mini" Quilt

Approximately 54" square

Materials Needed: 45"-wide cotton or cotton-blend fabric—3 yds. for backing, 1¼ yds. each cream for the blocks and solid red for the borders, hearts and binding; ¼ yd. each red print, green print and green solid for the hearts and leaves.

56" square of quilt batting.

Sewing thread to match the fabrics.

Cream or off-white quilting thread.

Cut two 25"-by-54" rectangles from the backing fabric; stitch them together along one long edge. From cream, cut four 22½"-square quilt blocks. From solid red, cut two side borders 5¼" by 44½" and top and bottom borders 5¼" by 54"; cut 2"-wide strips to piece four binding strips 55" long.

Make the blocks following the instructions for Block 25. Right side in, sew two blocks together so that the print corner hearts on one block are paired with the solid corner hearts on the other block. Repeat with the two remaining blocks, then sew the two pairs together along one long edge. Sew the side, then the top and bottom borders to the quilt.

Mark a large heart *(Template A)*, centered diagonally, in each corner of the border. Trace a large heart in the center of each border and halfway between the center and the corner. Trace the bow motif *(Template TT)* between each pair of hearts.

Assemble the quilt top, the batting and the backing *(see page 6)*. Outline-quilt the hearts in the blocks and borders; quilt along all marked lines.

Bind the quilt in red *(see page 8)*.

Hearts and Flower Wall Hanging

Approximately 20" by 54"

Materials Needed: 45"-wide cotton or cotton-blend fabrics—1½" yd. for the backing; 1 yd. white for the blocks; ½ yd. navy print for the borders and appliqués; ¼ yd. red pin-dot for the accent squares and the binding; scraps of yellow print, green print, red print, green pin-dot and gold solid.

22"-by-56" piece of quilt batting.

White quilting thread.

Sewing threads to match fabrics.

Embroidery floss—a few yds. each gold, four shades of blue and two shades of green.

Cardboard for templates.

This wall hanging is assembled in the traditional manner—assembling the blocks, lattice strips and accent squares, then adding the batting and back and quilting the entire piece using a hoop or frame, or in your lap.

From cardboard, cut templates for a 14"-square quilt block, a 3" accent square and a 3"-by-14" lattice strip. To use, trace around the template on the *wrong* side of the fabric. When cutting out the pieces, leave at least ¼" seam allowance around.

Trace and cut three quilt blocks from white, ten lattice strips from navy print and ten accent squares from red pin-dot. From red pin-dot, also cut 2"-wide strips and piece to make two 55"-long and two 21"-long binding strips. Cut 22"-wide strips of backing fabric and piece to measure 22" by 56".

Construct the blocks following the individual block instructions for Blocks 26–28. Arrange the three blocks in a row with a lattice strip between each pair of blocks and at each end of the row. Right sides in, matching the traced lines, stitch the blocks and strips together. Arrange three lattice strips end to end, with an accent square between each pair of strips and at each end of the row; stitch. Repeat with the remaining strips and squares. Right sides in, matching seams and traced lines carefully, pin a row of lattice strips and accent squares to the top and bottom of the row of blocks; stitch.

Baste the backing, batting and top together *(see page 6)*. Quilt the blocks as described in the individual block instructions; quilt around the lattice strips and accent squares ¼" from seamlines and ½" from raw edges.

Bind the wall hanging with red *(see page 8)*.

Don't feel that you must copy our projects exactly. These dimensions and techniques may be varied to suit your quilt size, fabrics and creativity.

Enjoy! And may you always have a happy heart!